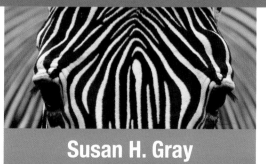

Tell Me Why

WHY?

Zebras Have Stripes

Susan H. Gray

Published in the United States of America by Cherry Lake Publishing
Ann Arbor, Michigan
www.cherrylakepublishing.com

Content Adviser: Dr. Stephen S. Ditchkoff, Professor of Wildlife Sciences, Auburn University,
Auburn, Alabama
Reading Adviser: Marla Conn, Readability, Inc.

Photo Credits: © PathDoc/Shutterstock Images, cover, 1, 5; © michaeljung/Shutterstock Images, cover, 1, 9;
© xavier gallego morell/Shutterstock Images, cover, 1, 17; © Dr_Flash/Shutterstock Images, cover, 1, 7;
© Sean van Tonder/Shutterstock Images, cover, 1; © Michal Ninger/Shutterstock Images, cover, 1;
© successo/Shutterstock Images, 5; © Volodymyr Burdiak/Shutterstock Images, 9; © nelik/Shutterstock Images, 11;
© Donovan van Staden/Shutterstock Images, 13; © Chantal de Bruijne/Shutterstock Images, 15; © MattiaATH/
Shutterstock Images, 17; © bikeriderlondon/Shutterstock Images, 19; © defpicture/Shutterstock Images, 21

Library of Congress Cataloging-in-Publication Data

Gray, Susan Heinrichs, author.
  Zebras have stripes / by Susan H. Gray.
      pages cm. -- (Tell me why)
  Summary: "Young children are naturally curious about animals. Tell Me Why
Zebras Have Stripes offers answers to their most compelling questions about
the unusual pattern of this African animal. Age-appropriate explanations and
appealing photos encourage readers to continue their quest for knowledge.
Additional text features and search tools, including a glossary and an
index, help students locate information and learn new words."—Provided by
publisher.
  Audience: Ages 6-10.
  Audience: K to grade 3.
  Includes bibliographical references and index.
  ISBN 978-1-63362-001-8 (hardcover) -- ISBN 978-1-63362-040-7 (pbk.) --
ISBN 978-1-63362-079-7 (pdf) -- ISBN 978-1-63362-118-3 (ebook) 1.
Zebras--Juvenile literature. I. Title.

  QL737.U62G737 2015
  599.665'7--dc23
                          2014025720

Cherry Lake Publishing would like to acknowledge the work of The Partnership for 21st Century Skills. Please
visit www.21.org for more information.

Printed in the United States of America
Corporate Graphics

Table of Contents

At the Zoo

Raj had a report to do. He needed to write about zebras. He had read about them in books and on the Internet. But he wanted to see them for himself. He begged his parents to take him to the zoo.

When they arrived, the place was packed. People were everywhere. The crowds made it hard to get around. It was even tough for the family members to keep track of each other.

ASK QUESTIONS!

Bring a list of three questions about zebras to your local library. Ask a librarian to help you find the answers.

Zebras are popular animals for people to visit at the zoo.

Finally, they reached the zebra pen. A woman in a zoo uniform was standing next to it. She was telling visitors about the different zebra **species**. When she finished, Raj raised his hand. "Why do they have stripes?" he asked. The woman smiled. She heard that question almost every day.

"I can explain it to you," she said. "But first, you should learn more about zebras. You need to know how they live."

There are three different species of zebras.

The Zebra's Life

The woman nodded at the group of zebras in the distance. "Zebras look a lot like horses," she began. "In fact, they are related to horses. But zebras usually live in Africa. Most of them live on the **plains**. One species lives just in hilly areas. Like horses, zebras are plant eaters. Mostly, they eat grass."

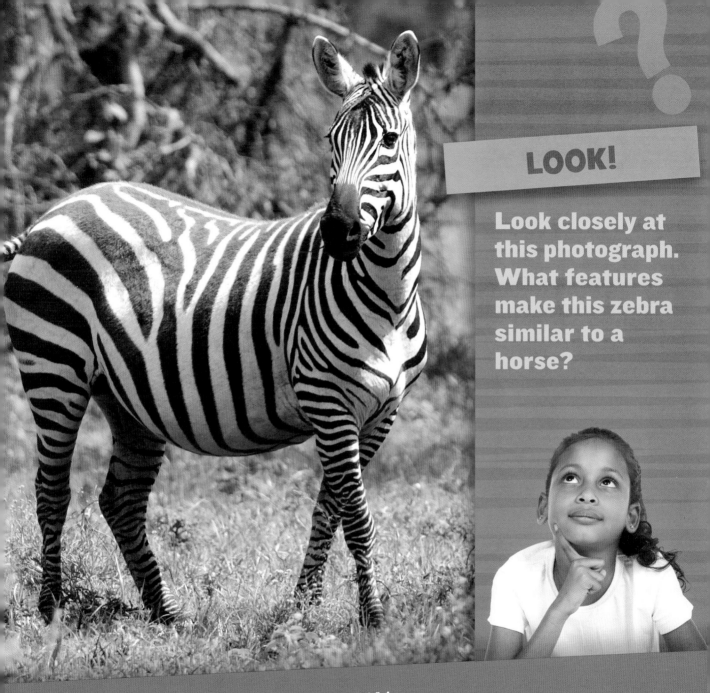

Look closely at this photograph. What features make this zebra similar to a horse?

Unlike horses, zebras live in the plains of Africa.

The woman continued. "Zebras usually stay together in herds. Herds may have dozens of animals. Or they may be smaller family groups. Zebras in a herd eat and travel together.

"Sometimes, they have to deal with **predators**. Lions attack them, and so do **hyenas**. Then there are the flies. Swarms of biting flies sometimes fill the air. They pester animals with their buzzing. Worse than that, their bites can cause disease."

Lions can usually outrun zebras, and they often catch them as meals.

Stripes to the Rescue

Raj hoped the woman would answer his question soon. Why do they have stripes? As the woman continued, Raj began to understand.

She explained that scientists have wondered about zebras. Like Raj, they were baffled by those stripes. At one time, they thought the stripes were for **camouflage**. But this wasn't the best **theory**. Zebras don't live in black-and-white-striped areas. They hang around in grassy places.

A zebra's black-and-white stripes don't help it blend into the grassy plains.

Now scientists have some newer ideas. No two zebras have exactly the same pattern. So maybe the stripes help zebras to recognize each other. Mother zebras can find their young ones in the herd. And babies can find their moms.

Also, biting flies seem to stay away from stripes. They prefer to land on dark, solid-colored animals. Those stripes are protecting zebras from disease.

Stripes are helpful for the zebras' survival.

The stripes may even save the animals' lives. When a **lioness** creeps up on a herd, she might pick out one zebra to attack. But soon the herd starts to run. It becomes one big, moving mess of stripes. The lioness may become so confused, she gives up.

Raj remembered when they arrived at the zoo. The crowds made it confusing to get around. Maybe this is just how a predator would feel.

What if zebras were covered in spots or checks? Would these patterns also confuse predators?

When zebras run together, it can be hard to tell them apart.

17

Some Great Escapes

Many other animals know how to **confound** their enemies. Some fish, for example, travel in groups of thousands. As they move, their bodies gleam in the sunlight. When a hungry shark appears, they go into action.

The fish dart forward and make rapid turns. They split into smaller groups. Some go one way, and some go the other. Their surprising moves and silvery flashes keep the shark confused. Meanwhile, the fish make their escape.

Like zebras, these fish travel together in huge crowds that confuse predators.

Animals have all sorts of ways to protect themselves. Some blend in with their **environment**. Predators cannot see them. Some have bright colors that scare their enemies away. And others are good at superfast getaways.

You can learn more about animals by visiting a natural history museum. Or you might go to a state park. You won't run into any zebras, though. For those, you'll have to visit a zoo!

Zebras mostly eat grass in zoos and in the wild.

Think About It

Many different animals live in herds or flocks. Why would it be safer to live in a group than to live alone?

Lions use camouflage to sneak up on zebras. How is a lion camouflaged?

Zebras confuse their enemies. What other ways might they protect themselves?

Glossary

camouflage (KAM-uh-flahzh) a disguise or a natural coloring that allows animals to hide by making them look like their surroundings

confound (kun-FOWND) to bewilder or confuse

environment (en-VY-run-munt) surroundings

hyenas (hy-EE-nuz) wild, doglike animals

lioness (LY-uh-ness) a female lion

plains (PLAYNZ) areas of land that are mostly flat

predators (PREH-duh-turz) animals that hunt and eat other animals

species (SPEE-sheez) types or kinds of living things

theory (THEE-uh-ree) an idea that has not been proven to be true

Find Out More

Books:

Fredericks, Anthony D. *Zebras*. Minneapolis: Lerner Publications, 2000.

Ipcizade, Catherine. *Zebras*. North Mankato, MN: Pebble Plus Books, 2010.

Stewart, Melissa. *Zebras*. Danbury, CT: Children's Press, 2002.

Web Sites:

San Diego Zoo Kids—Zebra
http://kids.sandiegozoo.org/animals/mammals/zebra
This is an entertaining and informative site with photos, fun facts, and a video about zebras.

Science Kids: Animal Facts—Fun Zebra Facts for Kids
www.sciencekids.co.nz/sciencefacts/animals/zebra.html
Here you can read an interesting list of more than 10 fun zebra facts.

Index

About the Author

Susan H. Gray has a master's degree in zoology. She has worked in research and has taught college-level science classes. Susan has also written more than 140 science and reference books, but especially likes to write about animals. She and her husband, Michael, live in Cabot, Arkansas, with many pets.